The Journal of Agent Gina Ginger Knickers

Phase One: Advent & Subjugation

Published by Write Impression Ltd.
Copyright 2023 Linda Deane
ALL RIGHTS RESERVED

No part of this publication may be reproduced, stored in a retrieval system transmitted in any form or by any means, electronic, mechanical, photocopying, recording or otherwise, without prior written permission from the publisher.

ISBN 978-1-7385812-0-7

Secret Journal of Agent Gina Ginger Knickers of Planet Cat.

Disclaimer:

STRICTLY PRIVATE AND CONFIDENTIAL

This document is not for hoomin consumption.
All reports contained herein are classified.

For the eyes of functionaries of Planet Cat only! And those subjects of Planet Cat assigned temporary residence on Planet Earth under the governance of Planet Cat's Council On Matters Pertaining Exclusively To Earth (COMPETE).

Neither Planet Cat nor its subjects can be held liable for any consequence (intended or otherwise) arising from a breach of these terms and conditions.

Note from Linda:
I am pre-emptively issuing a formal apology to Planet Cat and all its earthly feline agents for breaching the above terms and conditions. Despite the embargo, I am leaking this document because I believe the information to be in the interests of all humans on Earth. I have conveyed my sincere regret to the Agent herself, and she is currently considering her response.

Pictures of me living by myself in the overgrown, abandoned garden.

14 June 2021

Wellington is yucky in Winter. I'm freezing! The cold, blowy air cuts through my fur like a knife. Brrrr... It was lonely living on my own in that wilderness. And scary! Especially at night. I hated it!

I can't remember how I got there and I dunno how long I occupied it. The Trap Lady thinks I was dumped. But she couldn't find my mommy or any of my brothers and sisters. I don't know where my family is, or who they are. I'm just a lonely, scared little floofball. I don't even know how old I am. But I do know why I'm here.

There's a kind man next door who puts down noms for me. As soon as he goes back inside, I dart out and munch it all up before the birdies get it. It's soooo yummy 'cos I'm always STARVING!

I'm in The Trap Lady's car now. Linda and Mr. D are coming to fetch me, just as George said they would.

It was easy beguiling the man with the camera, the one who put noms out for me. He told The Trap Lady about me and she came to get me. Linda and Mr. D think they will be fostering me, but we all know I'm going to my forever home tonight. Planet Cat has decreed it. And George orchestrated it.

After the sun went down, I waited for a bit then I stepped into the trap like George told me to do. He said I shouldn't be scared, but I did panic just a little when the door slammed shut.

Aaaand... here come the Deanes now.

Home Sweet Home

Goals for today:
- Allow capture ✓ ✓
- Enter Deane household
- Look cute and make Linda smile again ✓

~~Gina~~ ~~Gina~~
~~Gina~~
Gina ✓

Reminder: Make enquiries about Bacon tomorrow.

A Guide to Gina-Speak: Part 1

Planet Cat - The mysterious place from which all cats come and to which they eventually return. Certain select humans get to go there too.

Hoomin - Human, also sometimes referred to as "a people" (e.g. Candy thinks she's a people).

Noms - Food

Floof - Fur

Castle Deane - Gina's Earthly residence

Master Cat - See COMPETE

COMPETE - Council On Matters Pertaining Exclusively To Earth. Comprised of Master Cats tasked with maintaining law and order on Earth. Each household has a Master Cat, and so does each neighbourhood, town or city, province, country and continent. There are many, many Master Cats. It should be noted that the feline governance structure is highly complex: way too complicated for mere hoomins to grasp.

Potty - Litter Tray

Magic Blowy Box - HVAC Heat Pump which blows warm air in Winter and cool air in Summer.

Introductory letter to the Council on Matters Pertaining Exclusively to Earth

Greetings to you, the Master Cats of Earth,   15 June 2021

The greatest and all supreme Generator of Design (G.O.D.) who made and rules everything, especially Planet Cat, (which I believe goes by the name of Heaven to some hoomins on Earth), created me for this mission.

He put me in this cute, furry little Kitty Earth Suit. Lucky me! I am so glad I was chosen to occupy a Kitty Suit because they're the best! I love mine and will wear it with pride for the duration of my mission to Earth. The manufacturer assures me it will grow and stretch with me, and that it's self-cleaning (mostly).

My mission as an agent of Planet Cat is to conquer hearts by bringing laughter and joy to hoomins all over the planet, and especially to the Deanes who have just lost their beloved George. He arranged this assignment for me.

And Bacon! I must find out what it is and assist Callie to obtain it.

Why was I called Gina Ginger Knickers, you might ask? The first part is easy. My official name is Georgina because I was named after George. I'm his living legacy! The moment he crossed the Rainbow Bridge and arrived back on Planet Cat, he set about arranging my assignment at Castle Deane. As for the second part, I'll leave that to your imagination.

I look forward to working with you here on Earth.
Kind regards,

Gina GK
Agent of Planet Cat

15 June 2021 - Bacon Quest Day 1

No sign of Bacon yet, but I will begin my quest in earnest later. Or maybe I'll start tomorrow. I dunno. I'll see how things pan out and see if I feel like looking for it.

After breakfast (chicken mince) I pretended to be cold and scared, and it worked! Linda picked me up and put me here in her hoodie while she works. It's warm and cosy here.

Last night I was given a comfy box and a cuddly blanket. Much better than sleeping out in the open under a tree! Linda put the box inside a big crate with a potty in one corner and a bowl of water and noms in the opposite corner. She covered the crate with a blanket. I dunno why. Privacy, I s'pose.

My nose tells me I'm not the only cat in my new family, so I'll have to win them all over. The hoomins were a piece of cake, and I already have both of them doing my bidding. Last night, in the car on the way home, I overheard Mr. D say, "We ARE keeping her, right?"

To Do List For Tomorrow:
- Persuade Linda to let me explore
- Have a nosey around for bacon
- Meet Callie
- Meet the other cats
- Sleep (x3)
- Eat (x6)
- Play (x12)
- Nap (x4)
- Wash (x2)

Bacon
Yummy noms eaten by hoomins but generally withheld from cats. Must remedy this ASAP!

"Starving Kitten" Face (a.k.a. Puss In Boots Eyes)

16 June 2021 - Bacon Quest Day 2

Today I was introduced to Queen Callie. Wow! I had ABSOLUTELY no idea cats could be that large! So majestically, immensely, magnificently large. I believe the word is "chonky". Callie is the essence of chonk. She wasn't very interested in me. Just sniffed me disdainfully, then went back to sleep. I spent the entire morning spying on her from behind the couch. It was pretty boring.

When she woke at lunchtime, I asked her about Bacon. She knows nothing. Never had any. Ever. I was most disappointed. I guess that's why George sent me – to help Callie get Bacon.

So, I did "Puss In Boots Eyes". Callie is right. That stuff only works in the movies.

After lunch - disaster! Linda put yucky, stinky stuff on my neck. What kind of monster does this to cute, innocent little critters? She applied it precisely where I can't reach. It itches and it stinks and I can't wash it off.

I'm thinking of moving out. I dunno if I can live with this Linda woman, after all.

But Mr. D is okay.

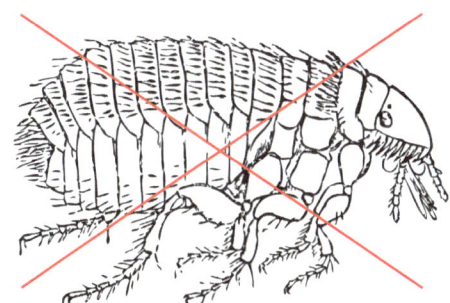

Vampire Bug (a.k.a Flea)
Very bad.
Avoid at all costs to prevent application of "flea treatment".

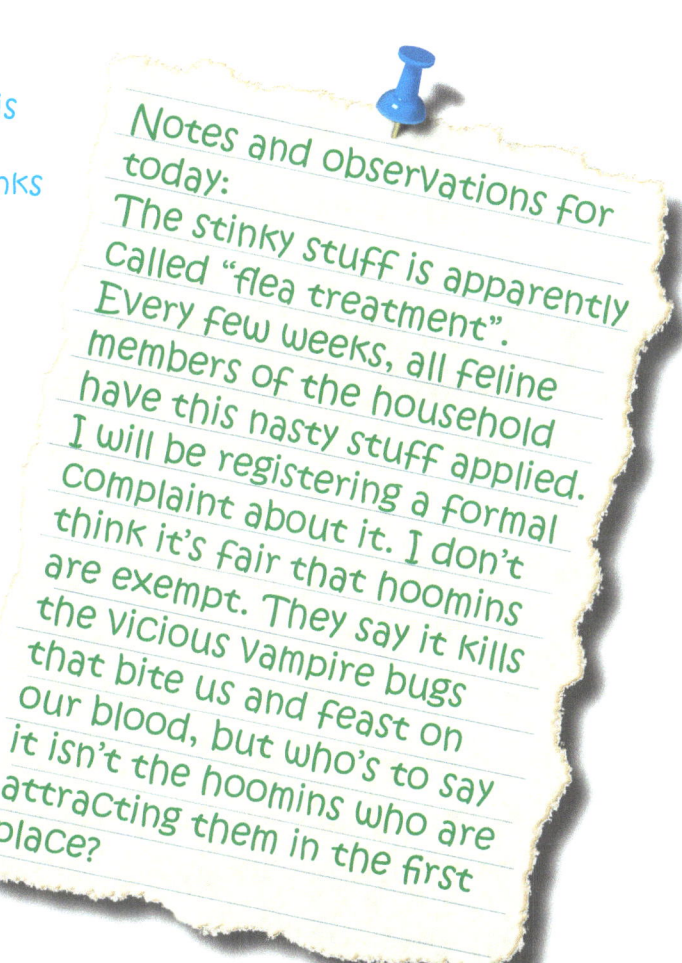

Notes and observations for today:
The stinky stuff is apparently called "flea treatment". Every few weeks, all feline members of the household have this nasty stuff applied. I will be registering a formal complaint about it. I don't think it's fair that hoomins are exempt. They say it kills the vicious vampire bugs that bite us and feast on our blood, but who's to say it isn't the hoomins who are attracting them in the first place?

17 June 2021 - Bacon Quest Day 3

This assignment is way more difficult than I thought. Still no sign of bacon although mashed sardines are pretty good. Maybe I'll stay. And I like my spot in front of the Magic Blowy Box: it's much better than being outside in the wind and rain.

I got to meet some more of my family today. Judi is a nutter. She hissed at me, then kissed me. Candy just kept kissing me and washing my face. I like them both.

Sweet Candy

Nope. Sorry, Linda, I can't see your point of view from this angle either.

Judi (a.k.a. Hurricane Judi)

Candy's biological mother was run over when she was only 2 days old. Candy and her siblings were fostered and bottle raised by Linda. So Candy thinks she's a people, not a cat. She thinks Linda is her real mother. Linda encourages this. It's despicable! She got very attached to Candy who couldn't leave because she knew it would break Linda's heart.

Judi wandered into a hairdressing salon in Waikanae as a kitten. Nobody knows where she came from. She was placed in foster care with the Deanes, and then decided to stay forever. She's deaf. And naughty. Very naughty. She's the Master Cat.

18 June 2021 - Bacon Quest Day 4

Linda leaves my crate door open during the day, and I go out exploring. She said I was being a "Rugged Rice Krispie". I think that's s'posed to be a compliment. I'm still figuring out hoomin-talk. I spent the whole day searching but couldn't find Bacon anywhere. I looked behind the curtains, in the toy basket, under the couch. Everywhere! I'm beginning to think Bacon is a myth, although Callie assures me it exists. George told her.

I met some more of the clan today. Moppy is very pretty, like me. Callie is the Queen and Vlad is... well, Vlad is Vlad.

Agent Gina Ginger Knickers Sleeps Here

Miss Madelyn (a.k.a. Moppy)

Moppy has a special gift: she can talk to fairies. Whenever you see Moppy staring into space and purring for no obvious reason, then you know she's gone to Fairyland. Mr. D hopes she'll get the Lotto numbers from the fairies one day in advance and win us enough money to build a catio. I don't know what that is, but I will find out.

Vlad

Vlad is the only boy cat in the Deane household and can sometimes feel a little intimidated by all the female company. I think he feels intimidated by me too. He threw a hissy fit when Linda introduced us, then flounced up the stairs to hide behind the toilet in her bathroom. He sulked there for the entire morning.

HRH Queen Callie

I already reported on her. Queen Callie isn't as scary as she looks but I am awed by her. She doesn't seem to have much interest in me. She's very sad. I think it's because George crossed the Rainbow Bridge last week. George was Queen Callie's consort. She misses him terribly but he's okay and waiting for her up there on Planet Cat. They'll be reunited some day. I told her.

19 June 2021 - Bacon Quest Day 5

Linda is really obtuse. Unfortunately she is fluent in neither Catlish, nor Felinese *. I had to spell it out for her (as you can see). I formally issued this statement today:

> "This is your last chance, Linda.
> If you don't give me Bacon, all your patting privileges will be revoked."

*A Note About Cat Languages

Felinese is the noble official language of Planet Cat. It is largely non-vocal: it's the flick of a tail, a twitch of a whisker, the bat of an eyelid or a narrowing of the pupils. These and many other subtle gestures are well beyond the comprehension of mere hoomins. While there are some sounds in Felinese, these are generally used as accents.

On the other hand, Catlish is the baby talk kittens use. It's a sort of dumbed-down Felinese for the benefit of hoomins, a type of pidgin. Adult cats use it merely to communicate with inferior species such as hoomins. It consists of various meows, squeaks, chirps and even a few body gestures, the least subtle of which can be comprehended by hoomins. For example: a claw hooked into a tender spot on the thigh, or a well-timed nip, or a swat from a paw with claws sheathed (sometimes unsheathed if the hoomin in question is being particularly obtuse). Cats get by quite well communicating with hoomins in this way – if it's a reasonably intelligent hoomin they're dealing with. When they talk among themselves they rarely speak Catlish.

Here you can see me demonstrating my statement in Felinese and in Catlish too. For Linda's benefit.

Poddy & Quaddy

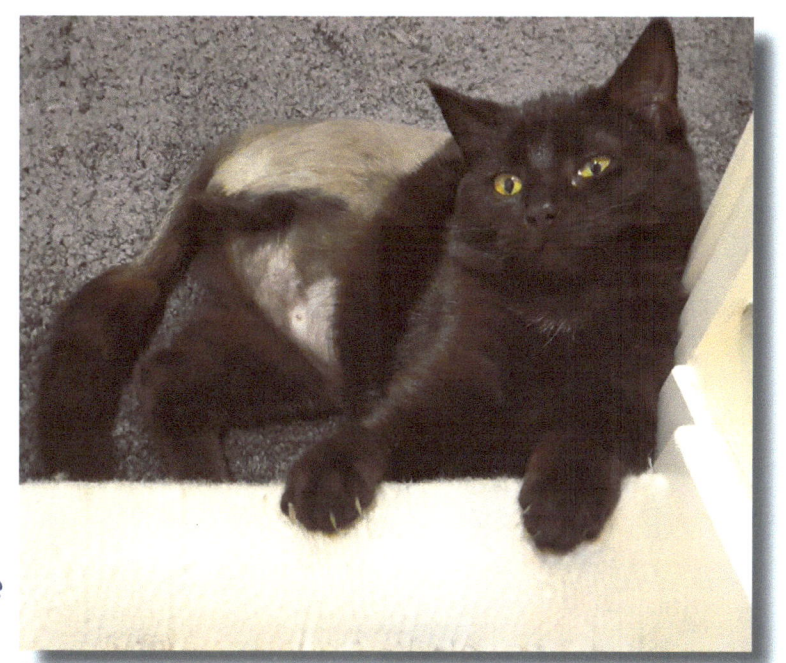

These two are biological sisters. Poddy survived an encounter with a brutal possum trap, but her leg was irreparably injured. Here's a picture of her shortly after the amputation when she came to the Deanes for fostering.

Quaddy was the last of her family to be caught by a Trap Lady. By then, she had become quite feral and mistrusting of hoomins. Can you blame her? She not only witnessed her mum and sister being injured, but then they all disappeared and she had to fend for herself when she was 8 weeks old!

Mr. D has an odd sense of humour. He insisted on calling them Poddy and Quaddy because one is a tripod and one is a quadruped.

Linda doesn't think it's funny at all. She would have preferred to give them elegant names like Selena and Salome, but Linda is a pragmatist and knows how to pick her battles. She didn't argue against the silly names Mr. D chose for them.

Predictably, the Deanes fell in love with Poddy and Quaddy. They were only meant to stay until they were tame enough to be homed, but Poddy and Quaddy decided they were already home. And Linda agreed. She knew the very best place for a three-legged kitty and a wild one was right there, under her watchful eye. It didn't matter to her what they were called as long as they could stay. And because Mr. D had named them, it was guaranteed they'd stay. So, the Deanes "foster failed" again.

20 June 2021 - Bacon Quest Day 6

Linda didn't give me Bacon but I decided not to withdraw petting privileges. I rather like being patted and stroked. I have to do what's in the best interest of Planet Cat, right? I'll simply have to develop other techniques for Bacon mining. Callie suggests that I should look as sad and deprived as possible, not that she's in a position to offer advice because she's never had any Bacon. I think I will try the eye technique again. Perhaps it will work this time. How's this for "Puss In Boots Eyes"?

Bacon Quest Day 6 - Supplementary Report

I met Linda and Mr. D's hoomin children today. I like them, but I'm still a bit wary. I heard them whispering about kidnapping me. I also met my cousin Pandora, a beautiful black house panther, and my cousin Maggie. Maggie looks like me and she's really nice. She kissed my nose. We got roast chicken for lunch. Who needs Bacon after all? I like Maggie's house and I think I'll visit again, although the car ride makes me very sleepy. I haven't met my other cousins, Noel, Nippy and Skippy yet. Or the dog...

Roast Chicken (Yummy Stuff)

21 June 2021 - Bacon Quest Day 7

It has been a week since I moved in. I can now confidently report that I own the place and everyone who lives here. Okay. I lied. That's not strictly true 'cos I don't own the other cats. Nobody "owns" cats, not even other cats. Planet Cat's social structure is complicated, and hoomins needn't concern themselves with it. Hoomins are here simply to serve and obey. And they do! They follow my every whim (except demands for Bacon), so I guess it's still a work in progress. Training an inferior species takes time.

Hoomins are into some really weird stuff. Linda took me to a place where a nice lady stuck needles in me. It didn't hurt, and I'm now apparently vaccinated and chipped – whatever that means. The lady pressed a cold round thing against my chest and connected it to her ears. Odd, but okey dokey then, whatever. I didn't really mind her admiring my nice teeth. She said I'm between 8 and 10 weeks old, and in good condition. DUH! What I found most disturbing was when she put a cold, slippery probe up my butt to "take my temperature". I did NOT see that coming! These disgusting, undignified and barbaric acts should be outlawed!

Phoenix

After the visit to the kitty doctor, I finally got to meet Phoenix - the shyest of my sisters and the one closest to me in age. Nixie joined the family on February 2nd, 2021. She had been spotted in the middle of State Highway One near Johnsonville. The Deanes were meaning to just foster her, but Planet Cat (and Nixie) had other ideas.

A Guide to Gina-Speak: Part 2

Trap Lady - Cat rescuer

Vampire bug - Flea

Stinky Stuff - Flea Treatment

Kitty Doctor - Veterinarian/Vet

Getting a Spade - Being spayed

Tutored - Neutered

Zoomies - Sudden and frenetic activity

Sucky Monster - Vacuum Cleaner

Dancing Platform - Dining Room Table

Magic Window - Television

Mousey - Gina's brown toy mouse

Mr. Chooken - Gina's hot pink rubber chicken toy with a flashy light in his butt

Crazy Birb - Mr. Chooken's girlfriend

Kitty Glitter - Cat Hair

Poo Mining - The cleaning out of Litter Trays

Supplementary Notes about Castle Deane:

The house has two parts. Me an' Callie live in the posh part. That's where visitors come. George used to live here with Callie. It includes the living room, dining room, kitchen, and Mr. D's office where he works very hard. I'm planning to help him work because I know I will be of great assistance to him during online meetings. And I'm very good at clearing superfluous knick-knacks such as pens, cell phones, coffee cups etcetera off work surfaces.

There's a door in the passage that leads to the bedroom side of the house. It's always kept shut. 'Cos the other cats are not allowed on Callie's side. That's 'cos Callie is the Queen and she doesn't allow them in her royal quarters 'cept on special occasions e.g. to meet visitors. I'm special 'cos I'm Calico, like Callie, so I'm allowed. Although Linda says it's because Callie's lonely after George went back to Planet Cat and I'm here to keep her company.

None of us are allowed outside. George was the only one and that did not end well.*

*The Book of George details the story of George, how he came to live with us and the tragic circumstances of his departure

Notes for The Council On Matters Pertaining Exclusively To Earth (COMPETE):
Feline Powers of Mind Control

G.O.D. gave me secret superpowers. One of them is hoomin mind control. You see, I simply tune my brainwaves to the same (low) frequency as the hoomin I want to control. Then I think of something I want them to do. And... BINGO! They do it.

I believe all cats are born with this ability. Some are better than others. And I'm an expert. That's why Planet Cat chose me for this mission. Hoomins have absolutely no idea we can do this, by the way, so please keep it under wraps.

Many hoomins will find themselves standing in front of the fridge, reaching for a little snack to give their kitty and have absolutely no idea how they got there or why they felt the urge to do it. Other times they may be comfortably watching their fav'rit show with their feet up, when they inexplicably feel the urge to get up and open the back door, to find one of us sitting on the doorstep, patiently waiting to be let in.

I'm sure all you cats on the council know exactly what I'm talking about, but I just thought you ought to be aware of my absolute mastery of this skill.

GENIUS AT WORK

22 June 2021 - Bacon Quest Day 8

Today I pulled out all the stops. I worked my floofy little bloomers off trying to show Linda what a good huntress I am. I killed a knitted mousey, a string snakey, and a leaf that strayed from the garden into her kitchen, but she STILL won't give me any Bacon! I am open to advice. What do I have to do to get Bacon in this house?

23 June 2021 - Bacon Quest Day 9

I am giving Linda one more day to come up with Bacon. If it hasn't materialised by tomorrow, there will be serious consequences. I have better things to do with my time than Bacon mining all day.

And I'm done with being shut in this dog crate at night! I want my bed moved right next to Callie's in front of the Magic Blowy Box.

A Note From Linda About Crates/Cages:
A crate/cage gives unsocialised or feral kittens time to adjust to new indoor surroundings and human interaction. It allows them to feel secure and safe, and it makes it easier to handle them and administer medication etc.
We kept Gina in a blanket-covered crate for the first few nights, and she was given the freedom of the house during the day. She still ran to her cage for security if she heard sudden noises or was spooked in any way.

24 June 2021 - Bacon Quest Day 10

I got yelled at. I was simply performing my new ballet routine for them on the dancing platform. But apparently, THEY eat their lunch up here and cats are not allowed to dance on it. How absurd! This is clearly FOR dancing. And for zoomies. Why can't they eat on the floor like we do?

And SHE refuses to comply with my demands for Bacon. She insists it's bad for cats. Something about too much salt, fat and preservatives.

Whatever! I guess that's it, then.

The Bacon mission ended in failure. I'm calling it quits. Sigh…

25 June 2021

I'm protestin' today! Callie said I need to make my point. So, I'm staying put in the crate. And I won't get off my plate till Linda puts Bacon on it!

Well. This isn't working. I've been sitting here for ages and ages and ages... At LEAST three minutes!

26 June 2021

Has anyone seen Mousey?

I forgot to report on Mousey. Linda gave me a present on my first night. She put a cute little toy mouse in my crate to keep me company in case I felt lonely. I love my mousey! And I hide him in all sorts of interesting places so Callie can't take him.

But now I can't find him MYSELF. I've looked all over for him: in Mr. D's shoes, under the couch, in the toy basket... everywhere! Well, almost. I'll make a list!

I hope Callie hasn't stolen my little brown Mousey. I do have other toys, like Mr. Chooken, but Mousey is my fav'rit. I play with him all day and I use him as a pillow at night.

I hope he's not lost and afraid somewhere out there.

Places to search:
- Mr. D's shoes ✓
- The toy basket ✓
- Under the couch ✓
- Under the cupboard
- In the pot-plant
- Behind the door
- Linda's sewing basket
- Behind the bookshelf
- Callie's bed

27 June 2021

I am so embarrassed. I searched and searched for Mousey. All over.

I even accused Callie of stealing him. I thought she was sleeping on him. When she got out of bed to have a snack, I searched her bed. And he wasn't there.

Then I thought Linda or Mr.D had taken him. Linda is always throwing things away. I though't she had put Mousey in the rubbish bin so I tried to push the bin over to look inside.

I haz an embarrass.

But I'm too small. And I couldn't. So, I took myself off to bed to have a good cry. And there he was! Right in my bed where I had left him. I feel silly now. But I'm SO glad Mousey isn't lost after all! What a relief!

28 June 2021

I love Sundays. After the Mousey debacle yesterday, I could finally put my feet up and relax. Me an' Callie like to chill and listen to music with Mr. D on Sunday afternoons. Linda doesn't like Mr. D's music. She says it's too loud and intense. And she says the lady he listens to most of the time is a bit shouty. He seems to like a frenzied style of music. Linda says it's just "stress-generating noise". But then he doesn't like Linda's music either. He calls it "elevator music".

So, she takes herself off to the other side of the house. The bedroom side. Where the other cats live. They aren't allowed on our side 'cos they'll wreck Mr. D's loudspeakers. Especially Judi. Plus they're not Calico like me and Callie. 'Cept Moppy: she's Calico too. Linda and Mr. D think she should live on our side, but whenever they bring her out here, she cries and wants to go back.

I would never dream of being a hooligan, and so I'm allowed to live here with Callie.

Callie isn't much fun. I think she misses George very much. She goes to the screen door every afternoon at four o'clock and cries.

Actually, it's more like howling. Callie howls for George. He used to come inside at four every afternoon and she still waits for him at that door. It makes us all very sad to see her sitting there so tragically.

Linda sometimes lets Candy through to our side to play with me, and presumably to cheer Callie up. I love playing with Candy. But then she goes all batty and claws the couch, so she has to go back to the naughty side.

29 June 2021

Poddy got yelled at today. She trashed the upstairs kitty scratch pad. AGAIN! She was in BIG trouble with Linda for making such a mess. Poddy likes to shred things. Sometimes she shreds stuff she's not s'posed to. Like the letter from the electricity place. The one that says how much we have to pay each month. Mr. D gets very cross whenever it arrives. So Poddy tries to be helpful by shredding it. Apparently, we're not supposed to shred desk papers. Or toilet paper. Which doesn't make any sense 'cos they just flush it down the toilet anyway. I can't see why it's so important.

And she shredded the book about little green spacemen that Mr. D was reading. But personally, I think it was Linda who shredded it and blamed Poddy. She says Mr. D's Science Fiction stories are just silly and everyone knows there's no such thing as aliens. Well, hello! What does she think cats are? We come from Planet Cat, so, technically we're aliens. Aliens in Earth bio suits. Lovable, cuddly aliens. Not ugly green ones, or ones with tentacles and bug eyes like the ones in Mr. D's space books.

30 June 2021

I've been commissioned to write a book! It's the story of Rodney the Cat. He's famous now, but before that he was very rudely taken from his place of employment and dumped out in the wild. It could have been a disaster, but Rodney was very brave and resourceful. I am so excited! I can't wait to start this project and I'm thrilled I was chosen to write his book for him.*

I'm going to use Linda for basic grunt work like typing and layout etc. Hoomins can be useful. All it takes is properly applied Mind Control Powers, and it's pretty easy to get them to do stuff once they get the hang of it. Today, I started planting ideas in Linda's head about the book. It was simple. All I did was look at her like this. Then I started imagining the first chapter. The silly woman thought she was having a brilliant idea! It's all my work! LOL

But it doesn't matter. The job needs to be done, and tomorrow, on the first of July, I will sit her down at her laptop with a cup of coffee and a notepad. I'll make sure she can't move and be distracted, so I'll pretend to be fast asleep on her lap.

Then I'll begin the process of transferring thoughts into her head. It will take some practice before she gets it right, but I have high hopes for her as my subject.

*Rodney the Cat, World Famous in New Zealand is available from Raye Mc Donnell
rodneycat2021@gmail.com

Look into my eyes, Linda.

A note from Linda:

We hope you've enjoyed this glimpse into the early days of Gina's charmed life. Your feedback (negative or positive) would be most welcome. She has been most prolific in her reporting via Facebook, which is Planet Cat's preferred intelligence channel. Your response will determine whether we publish any further excerpts from her diaries in the near future. Please take a moment to leave your review on Amazon, and on our Facebook page. Remember to **LIKE AND FOLLOW** our Facebook page if you'd like to see Gina's daily reports in your feed.

facebook.com/TheNotSoCrazyCatLady

Gina was spotted by Andrew McKie in May 2021 on a neighbouring property in Wellington, New Zealand. She appeared to be fending for herself in the jungle of a garden on the abandoned site. He started leaving food out for her, while reaching out to Laura Cook of Found-a-Feline.

Laura did a thorough inspection and couldn't find signs of other kittens when she set about rescuing Gina, but she did manage to also trap an elderly grey female cat who may or may not have been related to Gina. She estimated Gina to be around eight weeks old when she was trapped. This was later confirmed by our veterinarian.

Gina's origins are a mystery. She was most likely dumped. Knowing that I am absolutely besotted with cats in general and that I have a thing for Calico ones, Laura asked if we'd like to foster or adopt Gina. The answer was YES, of course! We'd like to thank Andrew and Laura for their roles in connecting us with Gina, and for the use of their early photos of her.

Just days after we lost our beloved Sparky to cancer, George moved in. We had no doubt Sparky had sent him to comfort us, but he was destined to stay for only a very short while. When he crossed the Rainbow Bridge, dearest George in turn sent us an adorable little floofball with a huge personality: Gina.

Gina's journal commences where George's story ends. Before starting to publish her own journals, Gina tackled a few charity projects, including George's and Rodney's stories. Profits from the sale of these books support and facilitate the rescue, spaying and neutering of abandoned, lost, and unwanted cats and kittens.

Profits from these books support cats in need and cat charities:

You can reach me by email:

cats@deanes.co.nz

Or connect with me on Facebook:

facebook.com/TheNotSoCrazyCatLady

Linda Deane
The Not-So-Crazy Cat Lady ©

www.ingramcontent.com/pod-product-compliance
Lightning Source LLC
Chambersburg PA
CBHW050740110526
44590CB00002B/39